Popular Cat Library

Maine Coon Cat

Abigail Greene

Published in association with T.F.H. Publications, Inc.,
the world's largest and most respected publisher of pet literature

Chelsea House Publishers
Philadelphia

CONTENTS

Popular Cat Library

Abyssinian Cat
American Shorthair Cat
Bengal Cat
Birman Cat
Burmese Cat
Exotic Shorthair Cat
Himalayan Cat
Maine Coon Cat
Persian Cat
Ragdoll Cat
Scottish Fold Cat
Siamese Cat

Publisher's Note: All of the photographs in this book have been coated with FOTO-GLAZE® finish, a special lamination that imparts a new dimension of colorful gloss to the photographs.

Reinforced Library Binding & Super-Highest Quality Boards

This edition © 1997 TFH Publications, Inc., 1 TFH Plaza, Neptune City, NJ 07753. This special library bound edition is made expressly for Chelsea House Publishers, a division of Main Line Book Company.

Library of Congress Cataloging-in-Publication Data

Greene, Abigail.
Guide to owning a Maine coon cat / by Abigail Greene.
p.   cm. — (Popular cat library)
Summary: A guide to the history, feeding, grooming, exhibition, temperament, health, and breeding of Maine coon cats.
ISBN 0-7910-5464-0 (hc.)
1. Maine coon cat Juvenile literature.   [1. Maine coon cat. 2. Cats. 3. Pets.]
I. Title. II. Series.
SF449.M34G74 1999
636.8'3—dc21
                                          99-26004
                                          CIP

HISTORY OF THE MAINE COON

Steeped in myth, folklore, conjecture, and fact, the Maine Coon has rightfully become one of the most popular cat breeds in America. It is one of the very few breeds that is truly American with perhaps a dash of Viking to add romance and intrigue into its ancestry. Believed for many years to be the result of a cross between a raccoon and a domestic feline or of matings between bobcats and farm cats, it is a breed that has all the hallmarks of mystery surrounding its origins.

Was the breed brought to America by the pilgrim fathers as they sought a new life in the colonies, or was it already roaming the countryside near Plymouth Rock, disdainfully watching the arrival of new human settlers into its domain? Then again, it could be a breed whose ancestors roamed the beautiful palaces of France during the reign of King Louis XVI.

If we rule out the impossible, we are left with the truth, which is a case of choosing between the options of probable or possible

Myths and legends surround the origin of the Maine Coon. At one time, the most popular of them held that the Maine Coon was the result of a cross between a domestic cat and a raccoon. Today we know, of course, that such a union is not possible. Owner, M. Weil.

but unlikely. In the years that preceded pedigree records, stud books, and organized breeding, nothing was cast in stone. This makes for calculated guesswork. It is this that adds the element of romance and mystery to the breed, for truth can at times be stranger than fiction. Is the present-day Maine Coon truly the cat of former years, or is it a look-alike created by breeders using available feline material?

THE MYTHICAL VIEWS

In the years preceding organized cat shows (the latter part of the 19th century), cats existed only as "types." No one really viewed them as anything special beyond the fact that they were there in the various guises of large, small, longhaired, or shorthaired. They were cute animals kept as pets by some people, though mostly they were retained in order to reduce the rodent populations around farms, houses, or commercial buildings.

They were essentially "working" creatures, much as were dogs and horses. The matter of how they arrived in a given place was not a subject of any great importance. As a consequence, all manner of stories circulated to answer this question should it be asked.

cats, though this fact in past years was not known by the average person. Genetics was in its infancy. All manner of believed animal crosses were accepted without question. Today, we know that a raccoon could not mate with a cat and produce offspring.

Red tabby Maine Coon. The most probable origin of this breed is a cross between a domestic New England house cat and an imported Angora. Owner, Karen Jacobus.

It was said that the Maine Coon was the result of hybridization between domestic shorthaired cats and raccoons. This explained the cat's ringed tail and use of its front paws to lift food items or play with water. Its hardiness to survive the harsh winters of Maine were bestowed on it from this tough carnivore.

The raccoon is a member of a totally different family (*Procyonidae*) than that of the

Another, though somewhat more believable, myth was that the Maine Coon resulted from crossings between domestic or feral cats and the bobcat (*Felis rufus*). This accounted for the tufts sometimes present on the ears of the Maine Coon. It also explained why this breed was larger than the average domestic feline. The fact that a bobcat would as readily eat a domestic cat than mate with it seems not to

Maine Coons are strong, agile cats. Red tabby with white Maine Coon owned by Betty Williams.

have been considered. Nor was it general knowledge at that time that many wild felines sported tufts to their ears, including those from which the domestic cat was derived — the small wild cats of Europe, Africa, and Asia.

Marie Antoinette loved dogs, birds, and cats — she had six Angoras. Her possessions and cats were placed on board the ship, but the Queen lost her head (literally!) before she could join them. The ship sailed, and the

The original color of the Maine Coon was tabby. Today Maine Coons are seen in just about every color and pattern, excluding pointed. Brown mackerel tabby owned by Hugh and Donna Richbourg.

THE FRENCH CONNECTION

With the myths dealt with, we can now examine a believable, if rather romantic, notion of the origins of the Maine Coon. It is said that during the French Revolution (c1788–1795) a plan was conceived to transport members of the royal family, including Queen Marie Antoinette, to the USA aboard the ship *Sally*. Its captain was a Samuel Clough of Wiscasset, a small coastal community south of Augusta, Maine.

Angoras arrived in America. There, it is said, they mated with local shorthaired cats and introduced the longhaired gene into the feline population.

From that royal start, the Coon cat, as it became known, developed in the following years. It is a touching story, but there is no proven record that it took place; although in the Wiscasset area, it would no doubt be hard to find an antique of that period which was not thought to have been owned by Marie Antoinette!

Although it is an old American breed, the Maine Coon did not gain recognition from US cat associations until 1967. Owner, Barbara R. Washburn.

A more plausible story is that a Captain Coon, who sailed between Maine and Europe during the 18th century, often returned with a number of longhaired cats. Maybe they were from Scandinavian ports and commanded good prices in the cold northeastern states of the US. Or perhaps, it was a case that many ships returned from such ports with hardy cats of the Nordic type, which is even more believable.

THE VIKINGS

An equally plausible theory places the Coon cat much further back in time than the 18th century. Vikings, the most feared European pirates of the 8th–11th centuries, are known to have established small outposts in Newfoundland and Nova Scotia long before Columbus or the pilgrims arrived in the New World. Leif Ericsson (1,000 AD) may well have taken tough, longhaired ship cats of Scandinavia with him on his expeditions.

A Norse coin made during the reign of Olav the Kyrre (1067–93) was discovered in Maine, and in recent years, there has been more proof of Viking activity in that state. We know these fierce seafarers took cats with them. These cats would have been the very hardy types typically seen, even to this day, in Sweden, Norway, and Russia.

When the Vikings departed, it is quite probable, indeed almost a certainty, that a number of the cats remained to live a feral existence and survived until the arrival of European settlers centuries later. If they had not survived, America would not have acquired one of the few populations of a truly pure breed type in the world. The process of domestication began all over again for kittens finding their way into the homes of the early pioneers.

Later, as the country became a focal point for European colonists sailing to the Americas to build a new life and nation, the influx of people, returning sailors, and their cats increased. This undoubtedly had diluted the pureness of any existing local feline stocks, but there is always the possibility that some of the cats in the more remote parts of the state remained untouched by this human and feline invasion until relatively recent times.

EARLY BREED HISTORY

In the centuries that followed the departure of the Vikings from America, there were no Europeans (that we know of) living in North America. When the pilgrim fathers arrived, they failed to note whether or not small cats of the European type were already to be seen. The cats they rarely referred to at all were those they took with them.

By the time the cat fancy was underway in the late 19th century, there were probably a million or more felines in the US. There were house cats, barn cats, and street cats. Included among these were the rugged cats of Maine. One of the first published references, specifically designed to the cats of that state, appears in *Book of the Cat* by F.R. Pierce and was published in about 1861. The cat mentioned in the book was a black and white longhair.

During the 1860s, Coon cats became the source of great pride in Maine. At county fairs, it became quite common for the best-looking examples to be exhibited for awards, and kittens were sold and taken to many parts of America. The most important show appears to have been that at Skowhegan, a town due west of Bangor. The top cats competed for the award of "Maine State Champion Coon Cat." The decade was one of great success for the Coon cat.

The harshness of the winters was the single factor that insured that only the fittest and most rugged survived. The local shows insured that the type remained true to the concept of what a Coon cat was all about, even though they were not judged against a written standard of excellence. During the next three decades that followed the 1860s, the Coon cat of Maine continued to prosper, but gray clouds were forming.

THE BEGINNINGS OF DECLINE

The event that marked the beginning of the decline for the Coon cat happened not in the United States but in Sydenham, London on July 13, 1871. It was in the Crystal Palace that Harrison Weir, now regarded as the Father of the Cat Fancy,

organized a cat show. It included numerous breed types — Persian, Siamese, longhairs, domestic shorthairs, Manx, and even a wild cat from Scotland. The show was an enormous success.

As a consequence, more and more cat shows were organized in Britain, each bringing to the attention of the public the considerable variety in types of cat known to exist in different parts of the world. In 1887, cat fanciers in Britain formed the National Cat Club and introduced stud books. The emergence of true "breeds" rather than "types" was underway. This was to have far-reaching effects on the highly popular Coon cat, the tough feline on the other side of the Atlantic.

In 1883, "The Grand Cat Show," America's first major cat show, was organized by the Boston Cat Club and held in Boston. It ran for two weeks, which was an incredible time span for any animal show in those days. In the show, as reported by the *Boston Traveler*, were "heavy cats, thin cats, old cats, Angora cats, Siberian cats, Coon cats, Maltese cats, and Tiger cats." In all, about 400 felines were exhibited.

The show was successful, and major shows continued to be held in Boston thereafter. In those of 1897, 1898, and 1899, Coon cats were still winning major awards. Following the first Boston show, an Englishman, J.T. Hyde, organized a show in 1895 in Madison Square Garden in New

Brown classic tabby Maine Coon. Owner, Jean Hannum.

York. He had visited the London show of 1871 and felt an exhibition based on the same format would be successful, which it proved to be.

The unexpected winner was Leo, a longhaired brown tabby cat from Maine. He proved prolific during the next few years, before one of his sons beat him in competition. It is worth noting that one of the cat fanciers at the New York show stated that although she was from Maine, her cats were not Coons. This clearly indicates that by 1895 breeders were already making distinctions between longhaired cats from Maine and the Coon cats of that state. The two types were similar but distinct.

The success of the northeastern shows in America was followed by great success at the Chicago show of 1898. Thereafter, more and more shows were held across America. What is abundantly clear, as the records are studied, is that in both Britain and the USA, the early days of the developing cat fancy were largely dominated by those in the upper classes — titled and monied people. Such people were greatly impressed by the magnificent longhaired Persians and Angoras. The exotic Siamese was another breed that quickly created an impact. The desire to own pedigreed Persians resulted in large numbers being shipped from England to the USA. It became fashionable to own British-bred cats. They had arrived in New York and Maine in the thousands by the turn of century.

The effect on the Coon cats of Maine was catastrophic. Who wanted a macho cat from the backwoods of the state when all the winners at shows were gorgeous Persians? If you were a cat breeder, it was profitable to breed fashionable rather than practical felines. Not surprisingly, many Coon cats were matcd to Persians and Persians to other longhaired cats present in the state.

The true intrepid Coon cat was becoming hard to find and losing ground every year under an avalanche of other fashionable breeds. There is nothing new in this scenario, for it has happened time and again in many animal hobby pursuits. Long established varieties go to the wall as new breeds become fashionable.

THE DESOLATE YEARS

As the 20th century got underway, times were hard for the Coon cats. By about 1904, few were being exhibited, yet in the first volume of the Cat Fanciers' Association (CFA) register, 28 Coons are recorded. The CFA was established in 1906 as the second of the American cat registries.

Today, it's the largest cat association in the world. During the opening years of the century, fewer and fewer Coons were exhibited — championship status was taken from them. None of the increasing number of national show societies accorded them this rank. It seemed that this magnificent cat would become a feline reject destined for extinction or, at best, to be relegated to the rank of barnyard cat from which it had emerged.

THE PENDULUM SWINGS

By the 1940s, it seemed that the halcyon days of the Coon cat from Maine were over, but the reality was that they had yet to begin. Though no longer a popular show cat and now in the ranks of the rare breeds, a number of dedicated fanciers still enthusiastically supported them in their home state. In 1953, they rallied and formed the Central Maine Coon Cat Club in Skowhegan. The club organized Coon-only shows, just as others had done during the 1860s.

In the following years, the breed slowly but steadily gained more and more admirers. A standard was drafted in 1967, and a year later, the Maine Coon Breeders and Fanciers Association was created. This provided more exposure and impetus to the breed's comeback. A number of the American registries began accepting registrations for the breed during the 1960s.

1976 proved to be a very important year for the Maine Coon because it was then that the CFA finally conferred championship status back to the breed. The pendulum had truly started to swing back in favor of America's first show cat.

THE PRESENT DAY

Today, not only is the Maine Coon the most popular longhaired breed in America after the Persian, but it also has spread to many other countries. The most notable of these is Great Britain. The nation that, so many years ago, started the system that would initially benefit the breed but ultimately almost destroy it, embraced the Maine Coon. It bestowed on the breed preliminary show status and a standard during the late 1980s.

For some years prior to this, the breed had a devoted following in Britain. It was through the efforts of such breeders that their Governing Council of the Cat Fancy (GCCF) accorded the breed official recognition. By 1989, the Maine Coon was Britain's 12th most popular breed. It was still a long way behind the Persian, Siamese, and Burmese, but ahead of the Angora — one of the breeds that had brought about the demise of the Coon cat in the USA during the late 1800s.

As a further irony of fate or fashion, the Siberian cat, the Russian equivalent to the Maine Coon, arrived in America in 1991 and is developing strong support. So too is the Norse Skaukatt, known in Britain and America as the Norwegian Forest Cat. In Sweden, the Racekatte and the Rugkatt of Denmark, both close cousins of the Maine Coon of the Viking period, are also enjoying a revival of their fortunes as popular exhibition felines.

It seems that you just can't keep a good cat down! However, I am sure that if you were to travel the back roads and forests of Maine you would sooner or later meet an aged farmer who would tell you, "Never mind those pampered show cats! If you want to see a *real* Coon cat, just have a look in my barn."

The Maine Coon has existed for as long as cats have been known in America. It still remains a breed for all tastes, such as the rugged farm cat that can withstand the extremes of bitter winters and is able to fend for itself or the charming feline that graces the show bench and can compete with the best of the Persians and the exotic breeds of Asia. It has survived the full spectrum of feline fashions and once again finds itself very much in the spotlight.

In its show-pen form, it may be more refined than its ancestors, but beneath its glamorous veneer still beats the heart of a true cat of the wilderness. It was shaped not by humans, but by the forces of nature in a state where only the strong could hope to survive — a feline of which those Vikings of so long ago would be truly proud.

It is interesting to note that the breed is, along with the Manx, Devon, and Cornish Rexes of Britain, the only breed of cat that is named for a relatively small geographic area. The transition in name from Coon cat to Maine Coon is reflective of the determination and pride among the devotees of the Coon cat to insure that the breed, which became so synonymous with the state of Maine, should forever into the future be associated with it no matter where it is bred.

The Maine Coon makes a good feline companion. It is active but not destructive. Owner, Frederick O. Duane.

MAINE COON CHARACTER

At times, the Maine Coon can be reserved, sometimes even aloof, but it won't hesitate to vocalize when the occasion calls for it! Owner, Robert and Patricia Cutrupi.

Affectionate, intelligent, aloof, playful, and curious are but a few of the words used by owners to describe the character of their Maine Coons. Of course, it can be said with justification that such words are equally applicable to all breeds. So in what ways does this rugged feline differ from the many other breeds from which you could choose?

A cat's character and traits can be broadly divided into four types. There are those that are common to all felines, which have evolved over thousands of years, or there are those that are breed related, like the ones that apply to dogs, horses, and other domestic variants of a wild species. Then there are those that are individual to the cat, and finally, there are those perceived by the owner. These are variable depending on the amount of interaction that takes place between owners and their feline companions.

With any breed trait, it is not so much that it is unique to the breed, but that it is repetitively common to the breed as a whole. A cat is indeed a cat, but a Siamese displays a very different collection of traits than a Persian or a Maine Coon. These two longhaired breeds share a number of characteristics, yet are very different in others.

A STOIC BREED

Being a breed of old ancestry that derives from the hardy cats of Europe rather than those of Eastern countries, the Maine Coon is all of the things that can be regarded as stoic. It is a serious, dignified, and pensive breed without being in any way heartless or uncaring. Actually it is quite the opposite — extremely affectionate. However, its affection may be restricted to just a few people, like its family, with whom it has an intimate relationship. To outsiders, it can appear rather indifferent, as though it is deeply suspicious of them.

This does not mean that all Maine Coons display this stoic nature. The individuality of the cat is shaped to a great extent by the environment it is reared in and the number of people it meets in its day-to-day life. Nonetheless, it can be said that it is a breed that has a predisposition to being cautious about whom it will trust and regard as a friend.

A HARDY BREED

While many modern-day breeds have been dramatically changed from our notion of what a hardy cat is all about, this does not apply to the Maine Coon. It remains, thankfully, what it always was. It is a breed unfettered by genetic mutations or breeder fashions, which have made some breeds susceptible to many physical weaknesses. Consider the problems of the button nosed Persians, the back problems of the Manx, or the skin problems related to the Sphynx. Even the Siamese is only a shadow of the hardy and beautiful archetypal cat of that name.

The Maine Coon has no inherent problems, no association with birthing difficulties, no anatomical weakness, and no inability to cope with the changing weather seasons. It is hardy in physical strength as well. This is not a breed, especially the males, to run away when there is a cat fight in the making. As a large breed, it has lost none of its ability to look after itself if the need arises. Breeders have successfully striven to maintain the very traits that enabled it to live an almost feral existence all those years ago in the rugged winter climates of its home state.

Originally a working cat, the Maine Coon is solid and rugged. Owner, Sharon Behringer.

The Maine Coon's coat enables it to cope with the changing seasons: in winter, it is thick and full to protect against the cold; in summer, it will thin out to provide relief from the heat. Owner, Frederick O. Duane.

A QUIET BREED

The Maine Coon, other than when in the mood for breeding, is not an excessively vocal cat in the sense of being noisy. It does chirp a lot, especially when holding a conversation with its closest human companions. This said, when these cats do give of their voice, you will be very aware of it. Like wild cats, they prefer silence until they really have something to say — then they do it in style.

NOT THE FLAMBOYANT FELINE

Unlike the foreign breeds, which are very flamboyant and mischievous, the Maine Coon, like most longhaired breeds, is more demure in its day-to-day life. A romp up your velvet drapes just for the fun of it or a walk along shelves taking delight in knocking everything to the floor is not for them. A kitten may test its claws and paws with such pranks, but the breed matures to be more sedate.

It may have the occasional "mad moments" when it will run around the home, but generally, it is a no-nonsense breed that would rather sit on the window sill contemplating the antics of others inside or outside its home. It is a relaxed breed that sees no point in expending energy, unless there is a really worthwhile objective, like traveling to its food dish or chasing a bird. This does not mean it has no interest in playing games but can generally be relied upon not to cause havoc while you are away.

IDIOSYNCRASIES

A trait many Maine Coon owners attest to is that the breed often raises itself on its haunches to view things not seen at ground level, which is unusual for a large, longhaired feline. It is reminiscent of a rabbit or raccoon. This action is more commonly associated with the slimly built foreign breeds.

Another trait this breed displays is the enjoyment of greeting its owners with head-to-head rubbing. Many breeds will rise on their hind legs and butt the hand of their owner, but Maine Coons like to jump onto something so they can butt their head against their owner's chin or forehead, much in the manner they would greet other cats. They will also do this when they are sitting on their owner's lap, pushing up to butt their chin in order to gain extra attention.

INTELLIGENT SENSITIVITY

The natural intelligence of this breed enables it to quickly sense the mood of its owner, though it must also be said that they can sometimes be demanding at the wrong moment. Their mental prowess often gives them a disdainful look, as though they are aloof and somewhat contemptuous of humans. Possibly they are! However, they simply have a very dignified demeanor that is easily misinterpreted by those not familiar with the breed.

That they are not arrogant is clearly shown by their very affectionate nature. As a natural breed, their wildness has long since given way to a confiding and gentle disposition, at least with those they love.

Who then will make the ideal companion to a Maine Coon? It is not always prudent to place either people or cats into "pigeon holes," but generally, the breed will be well-suited to those who are not looking for a mischievous, cheeky sort of feline. It is more a cat that blends into the surroundings without making any noise or fuss to draw attention to itself.

If you are the quiet, studious, stay-at-home type and are looking for a similar companion happy to lay on your lap or next to you, the Maine Coon could be the ideal choice. It will suit families where the children are more mature and able to appreciate the virtues of this very refined and imposing breed.

One thing that any Coon cat owner should be aware of is that the breed will require very regular grooming. As much as you might love to own one of these beautiful felines, unless you are prepared to devote time to this requirement, you should admire rather than own this or any longhaired breed.

Silver classic tabby with white. The pale, clear silver ground color is accentuated by dense black markings. Owner, Connie Webb.

This show-quality white Maine Coon is exhibiting play posture. If it were angry, its claws would be extended. Owner, Thomas and Suzanne Shambaugh.

THE MAINE COON STANDARD & COLORS

In order to determine the relative quality of a Maine Coon cat, or any other feline, there must be a standard against which the individual can be compared. The standards are prepared by a panel of experts within each cat registration body. Periodically these descriptive documents are amended to take account of progress within the breed, or to place more emphasis on a given aspect that may be regressing. The standard can never be precise, so is open to interpretation.

Like other cats, your Maine Coon will have a favorite spot in the house. Cats like places that are above ground level and enable them to watch what's going on below.

Within each standard, points are allocated to various features based on their believed importance within the breed. Any person who has aspirations to exhibit, judge, or breed Maine Coons should have a knowledge of the standard. Only by constantly referring to it can a mental picture be developed of an outstanding Maine Coon.

To the beginner almost any Maine Coon would seem to be a fine example when they compare it to the standard. The interpretation of the standard becomes meaningful only when combined with the experience of viewing poor, through mediocre, to those adjudged to be outstanding examples of the breed.

THE MAINE COON STANDARD

The standard quoted in this text is that of the Cat Fanciers' Association of America (CFA) and is reproduced by courtesy of that Association. The CFA is the largest registration organization in the US and the one most Americans will join.

In Great Britain, there are only two registration bodies and of them the Governing Council of the Cat Fancy (GCCF) is easily the most important, and is also the oldest registry in the world.

If you plan to breed Maine Coons, you are strongly recommended to do so only with registered individuals. You should obtain the show standards for the registry you plan to support. The standards are not reproduced individually but within booklets that cover all breeds recognized by the registry in question.

Point Score of the CFA

Head (30)

Shape 15
Ears 10
Eyes 5

Body(35)

Shape 20
Neck 5
Legs and Feet 5
Tail 5
Coat 20

Color (15)

Body color 10
Eye color 5

The Maine Coon is a hardy breed of cat that throughout the ages has withstood New England's cold climate and rugged terrain. Brown tabby with white owned by Betty Williams.

General: Originally a working cat, the Maine Coon is solid, rugged, and can endure a harsh climate. A distinctive characteristic is its smooth, shaggy coat. With an essentially amiable disposition, it has adapted to varied environments.

Another myth about the Maine Coon's origins is that it was the result of a cross between a domestic cat and a bobcat. This was probably due to the fact that the Maine Coon bears a resemblance to the bobcat, most notably, the tufted ears. Owner, Barbara R. Washburn.

Head shape: Medium in width and medium long in length with a squareness to the muzzle. Allowance should be made for broadening in older studs. Cheekbones high. Chin firm and in line with nose and upper lip. Nose medium long in length; slight concavity when viewed in profile.

Ears: Large, well-tufted, wide at base, tapering to appear pointed. Set high and well apart.

Eyes: Large, expressive, wide set. Slightly oblique setting with slant toward outer base of ear.

Neck: Medium long.

Body shape: Muscular, broad chested. Size medium to large. Females generally are smaller than males. The body should be long with all parts in proportion to create a well-balanced rectangular appearance with no part of the anatomy being so exaggerated as to foster weakness. Allowance should be made for slow maturation.

Legs and feet: Legs substantial, wide set, of medium length, and in proportion to the body. Paws large, round, well-tufted. Five toes in front; four in back.

Tail: Long, wide at base, and tapering. Fur long and flowing.

Coat: Heavy and shaggy; shorter on the shoulders and longer on the stomach and britches. Frontal ruff desirable. Texture silky with coat falling smoothly.

Penalize: A coat that is short or overall even.

The body of the Maine Coon is long with all parts in proportion, creating a well-balanced rectangular appearance. Female members of the breed are generally smaller than their male counterparts. Owner, Thomas and Suzanne Shambaugh.

The Maine Coon's head is medium in width and medium long in length with a squareness to the muzzle. Owner, Judy Friedman.

The ears are large, well-tufted, wide at the base, and tapering to appear pointed. Owner, Evelyn Rae Powers.

Disqualify: Delicate bone structure. Undershot chin. Crossed eyes. Kinked tail. Incorrect number of toes. Buttons, lockets, or spots.

MAINE COON CAT COLORS

Eye color: Eye color should be shades of green, gold, or copper, though white cats may also be either blue or odd-eyed. There is no relationship between eye color and coat color.

Solid Color Class

White: Pure glistening white. *Nose leather and paw pads*: pink.

Black: Dense coal black, sound from roots to tip of fur. Free from any tinge of rust on tips or smoke undercoat. *Nose Leather*: black. *Paw pads*: black or brown.

Blue: One level tone from nose to tip of tail. Sound to the roots. *Nose leather and paw pads*: blue.

Red: Deep, rich, and clear brilliant red; without shading, markings, or ticking. Lips and chin the same color as coat. *Nose leather and paw pads*: brick red.

Cream: One level shade of buff cream, without markings. Sound to the roots. *Nose leather and paw pads*: pink.

Tabby Color Class

Classic tabby pattern: Markings dense, clearly defined, and broad. Legs evenly barred with bracelets coming up to meet the body markings. Tail evenly ringed. Several unbroken necklaces on neck and upper chest, the more the better. Frown marks on

A distinctive characteristic of the Maine Coon is the heavy, shaggy coat. Owner, Richard Weiss.

forehead form an intricate letter "M." Unbroken line runs back from outer corner of eye. Swirls on cheeks. Vertical lines over back of head extend to shoulder markings, which are in the shape of a butterfly with both upper and lower wings distinctly outlined and marked with dots inside outline. Back markings consist of a vertical line down the spine from butterfly to tail with a vertical stripe paralleling it on each side, the three stripes well separated by stripes of ground color. Large solid blotch on each side to be encircled by one or more unbroken rings. Side markings should be the same on both sides. Double vertical rows of buttons on chest and stomach.

Mackerel tabby pattern: Markings dense, clearly defined, and all narrow pencillings. Legs evenly barred with narrow bracelets coming up to meet the body markings. Tail barred. Necklaces on neck and chest distinct, like so many chains.

Head barred with an "M" on the forehead. Unbroken lines running back from the eyes. Lines running down the head to meet the shoulders. Spine lines run together to form a narrow saddle. Narrow pencillings run around the body.

Patched tabby pattern: A patched tabby (torbie) is an established silver, brown, or blue tabby with patches of red and/or cream.

Silver tabby (classic, mackerel, patched): Ground color pale, clear silver. Markings dense black. White trim around lip and chin

allowed. *Nose leather*: brick red desirable. *Paw pads*: black desirable.

Blue-silver tabby: Ground color pale, clear silver. Markings a deep blue affording a good contrast with ground color. White trim around lip and chin allowed. *Nose leather*: old rose desirable. *Paw pads*: rose desirable.

Red tabby (classic, mackerel): Ground color red. Markings deep, rich red. White trim around lip and chin allowed. *Nose leather and paw pads*: brick red desirable.

Brown tabby (classic, mackerel, patched): Ground color brilliant coppery brown. Markings dense black. Back of leg black from paw to heel. White trim around lip and chin allowed. *Nose leather and paw pads*: black or brown desirable.

Blue tabby (classic, mackerel, patched): Ground color pale bluish ivory. Markings a very deep blue affording a good contrast with ground color. Warm fawn overtones or patina over the whole. White trim around lip and chin allowed. *Nose leather*: old rose desirable. *Paw pads*: rose desirable.

Cream tabby (classic, mackerel): Ground color very pale cream. Markings of buff or cream sufficiently darker than the ground color to afford good contrast but remaining within the

Eye colors in the Maine Coon are green, gold, or copper, although white cats may also be blue eyed or odd eyed.

dilute range. White trim around lip and chin allowed. *Nose leather and paw pads*: pink desirable.

Cameo tabby (classic, mackerel): Ground color off-white. Markings red. White trim around lip and chin allowed. *Nose leather and paw pads*: rose desirable.

Tabby with White Class

Tabby with white: Color as defined for tabby with or without white on the face. Must have white on bib, belly, and all four paws. White on one-third of body is desirable. Colors accepted are silver, red, brown, blue, cream, and cameo.

Van tabby: White with color confined to the extremities: head, tail, and legs. One or two small colored patches on body allowable. Tabby pattern to be present in the colored markings.

Patched tabby with white (torbie with white): Color as described for patched tabby (torbie) but with distribution of white markings as described in tabby with white. Color as described for patched tabby (torbie) with or without white on face. Must have white on bib, belly, and all four paws. White on one-third of body desirable. Colors accepted are silver, brown, or blue.

Blue-silver tabby and white: Color as defined for tabby with or without white on the face. Must have white on bib, belly, and all four paws. White on one-third of the body is desirable.

Maine Coon kittens experience a remarkable growth rate and are fairly large by the age of four to eight months.

Parti-color Class

Tortoiseshell: Black with unbrindled patches of red and cream. Patches clearly defined and well broken on both body and extremities. Blaze of red or cream on face is desirable.

Tortoiseshell with white: Color as defined for tortoiseshell with or without white on the face. Must have white on bib, belly, and all four paws. White on one-third of body is desirable.

Calico: White with unbrindled patches of black and red. White predominant on underparts.

Dilute calico: White with unbrindled patches of blue and cream. White predominant on underparts.

Blue-cream: Blue with patches of solid cream. Patches clearly defined and well broken on both body and extremities.

Blue-cream with white: Color as defined for blue-cream with or without white on the face. Must have white on bib, belly, and all four paws. White on one-third of the body is desirable.

Bi-color: A combination of a solid color with white. The colored areas predominate with the white portions being located on the face, chest, belly, legs, and feet. Colors accepted are red, black, blue, and cream.

Van bi-color: White with color confined to the extremities: head, tail, and legs. One or two small colored patches on body allowable.

OTHER MAINE COON COLORS CLASS

Chinchilla silver: Undercoat pure white. Coat on back, flanks, head and tail sufficiently tipped with black to give the characteristic sparkling silver appearance. Legs may be slightly shaded with tipping. Chin, ear tufts, stomach, and chest, pure white. Rims of eyes, lips, and nose outlined with black. *Nose leather:* brick red. *Paw pads:* black.

Shaded silver: Undercoat white with a mantle of black tipping shading down from sides, face, and tail from dark on the ridge to white on the chin, chest, stomach, and under the tail. Legs to be the same tone as the face. The general effect to be much darker than a chinchilla. Rims of eyes, lips, and nose outlined with black. *Nose leather:* brick red. *Paw pads:* black.

Shell cameo (red chinchilla): Undercoat white, the coat on the back, flanks, head, and tail to be sufficiently tipped with red to give the characteristic sparkling appearance. Face and legs may be very slightly shaded with tipping. Chin, ear tufts, stomach, and chest, white. *Nose leather, rims of eyes, and paw pads:* rose.

Shaded cameo (red shaded): Undercoat white with a mantle of red tipping shading down the sides, face, and tail from dark on the ridge to white on the chin, chest, stomach, and under the tail. Legs to be the same tone as face. The general effect to be much redder than the shell cameo. *Nose leather, rims of eyes, and paw pads:* rose.

Black smoke: White undercoat, deeply tipped with black. Cat in repose appears black. In motion, the white undercoat is clearly

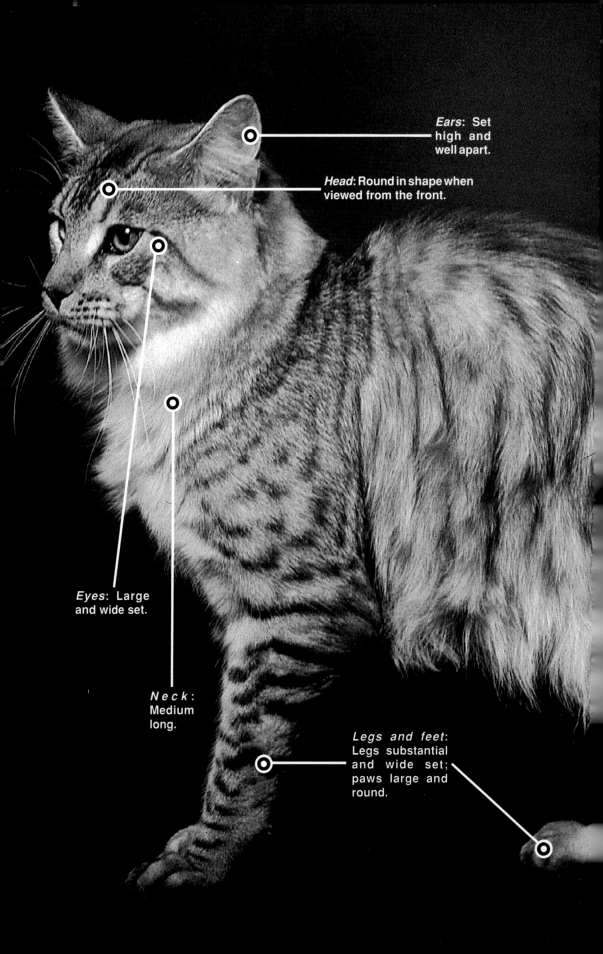

Ears: Set high and well apart.

Head: Round in shape when viewed from the front.

Eyes: Large and wide set.

N e c k: Medium long.

Legs and feet: Legs substantial and wide set; paws large and round.

Body: Muscular and broad chested.

Tail: Long, wide at base, and tapering.

apparent. Points and mask black with narrow band of white at the base of hairs next to the skin, which may be seen only when fur is parted. Light silver frill and ear tufts. *Nose leather and paw pads*: black.

Blue smoke: White undercoat, deeply tipped with blue. Cat in repose appears blue. In motion, the white undercoat is clearly apparent. Points and mask blue with narrow band of white hairs next to the skin, which may be seen only when fur is parted. White frill and ear tufts. *Nose leather and paw pads*: blue.

Cameo smoke (red smoke): White undercoat, deeply tipped with red. Cat in repose appears red. In motion, the white undercoat is clearly apparent. Points and mask red with narrow band of white at base of hairs next to the skin, which may be seen only when fur is parted. *Nose leather, rims of eyes, and paw pads*: rose.

Blue-cream smoke: White undercoat, deeply tipped with blue, with clearly defined patches of cream as in the pattern of the blue-cream. Cat in repose appears blue-cream. In motion, the white undercoat is clearly apparent. Face and ears blue-cream pattern

The Maine Coon's coat is shorter on the shoulders and longer on the stomach and britches. Owner, Dean Mastrangelo.

with narrow band of white at the base of the hairs next to the skin, which may be seen only when the fur is parted. White ruff and ear tufts. Blaze of cream on face is desirable.

Tortie smoke: White undercoat, deeply tipped with black with clearly defined unbrindled patches of red and cream. Cat in repose appears tortoiseshell. In motion, the white undercoat is clearly apparent. Face and ears tortoiseshell pattern with narrow band of white at the base of the hairs next to the skin, which may be seen only when parted. White ruff and ear tufts. Blaze of red or cream on face is desirable.

Smoke with white: Color as defined for smokes with or without white on the face. Must have white on bib, belly, and all four paws. White on one-third of the body is desirable.

OMCCC (Other Maine Coon Cat Colors): Any other color with the exception of those showing hybridization resulting in the colors chocolate, lavender, the Himalayan pattern, or these combinations with white.

Maine Coon Cat allowable outcross breeds: none.

As a Maine Coon kitten matures, its fluffy kitten coat will be replaced by a heavy coat. Owner, M. Soble and M. Thompson.

SELECTING A MAINE COON CAT

Before discussing the matter of selecting a Maine Coon Cat or kitten, it is appropriate to offer a cautionary note. The Maine Coon is a singularly beautiful feline with a magnificent coat. However, this coat is not self-grooming! If left unattended the Maine Coon can look a very sorry example of a cat. The fur will mat right down to the skin. The extent of the mats will become greater every time your pet gets wet. If you are not prepared to devote 20 or so minutes every few days to grooming your Maine Coon, then do not obtain an example of this breed (or indeed any longhaired breed). If you plan to exhibit your Maine Coon, it will need grooming daily to ensure the coat remains in the best condition.

THE QUALITY OF YOUR PET

Maine Coons come in a range of qualities from the inferior, through the typical examples of the breed, to those which are show winners, or at least potentially so. You may wish to own a high-quality Maine Coon even though you have no intention to show it. Quality means it will have good bone conformation, the correct stature, and its color or patterns will be of a high standard. Such a cat will be a costly purchase. A typical

Maine Coons need regular grooming to keep their coats looking their best.

Do your homework before you choose your Maine Coon: visit shows and talk to exhibitors. The more Maine Coons you see, the more likely you are to make the right choice. Owner, Karen Jacobus.

Maine Coon will be just that. It will display no glaring faults and its color will be sound. It may display some minor failings in type or color that would preclude it from ever being of show quality.

An inferior Maine Coon will be one which has obvious faults, either its conformation, its coat quality, poor color or in other ways inferior. Such cats are often described as being pet quality. As long as you appreciate that this term means inferior, its use is fine. However, there are two kinds of inferior Maine Coons. There is the cat which is inferior only in respect to its type and color—not in relation to its basic structure and health.

There is then the inferior cat produced by those who are in Maine Coons just to make money. These people have cats that they breed with no consideration for the vigor of the offspring. Such kittens are invariably sickly and prone to illnesses throughout their lives. Poor health and inferior Maine Coons result from unplanned matings and excessive breeding, coupled with a lack of ongoing selection being applied to future breeding stock.

How do you make the right choice when selecting a Maine Coon? The answer is you do your homework. Visit shows, talk to established exhibitors, and judges. When you visit the seller take a good look at his stock, and more especially the living conditions of the cats. Is he giving you the hard sell, or does he seem more concerned about the kitten's future home? Sometimes the dedicated seller might even annoy you, but he is concerned for his kittens, even if they are not quality Maine Coons. The more Maine Coons you see, the more likely you are to make a wise choice.

WHICH SEX TO PURCHASE?

From the viewpoint of pet suitability, there really is no difference between a tom (male) and a queen (female). Some people prefer one sex, but this is purely subjective. This author has found males to be more consistent in their character than females, who may tend to be "all or nothing" in their attitude. In other words, they can be extremely affectionate one day, but rather standoffish the next. The tom tends to be much the same from one day to the next, whatever his character might be.

It really is a pot-luck matter just how affectionate a kitten will grow up to become. Cats are very much individuals, and they can change as they grow up. The way they are treated also affects their personality. Therefore, it is more a case of selecting a kitten that appeals to you, regardless of its sex.

Of course, if you wish to become a breeder then the female has to be the better choice. Once she reaches breeding age you can then select a suitable mate for her from the hundreds of quality stud

males available to you. If you purchase a male with the view to owning a stud, you are really gambling that he will mature into a fine cat that others would want to use. For this to happen, your tom would need to be very successful in the show ring, and then in the quality of his offspring.

Furthermore, owning a whole tom (a male that has not been neutered) does present more practical problems than owning a queen. Such a male will be continually marking his territory (your furniture) by spraying it with his urine, which is hardly a fragrant scent!

If your Maine Coon is to be a pet only, then regardless of the sex you should have it neutered or spayed. It will be more affectionate to you, will not be wandering off looking for romance, and will not shed its coat as excessively as would an unaltered Maine Coon. In the case of a tom, he will not come home with pieces of his ears missing as a result of his fights with other entire males. Your queen will not present you with kittens that you do not want but which she will have if she is not spayed. She is far less likely to spray than is the male, but she will show her desire to mate, both with her "calling" sounds, which can be eerie, and her provocative crouching position in which she is clearly inviting a mating.

WHAT AGE TO PURCHASE?

Breeders vary in the age they judge a kitten ready for a new

A cat carrier is the ideal way to transport your new kitten home. Line it with a towel or blanket for added comfort. Owner, Susan E. Shaw.

home. An important consideration is obviously if the new owners have experience of cats generally and kittens in particular. While an eight-week-old baby is quite delightful, it is invariably better from a health standpoint that the kitten remains with its mother until it is ten or more weeks of age. Some breeders will not part with a kitten until it is 16 weeks of age.

The kitten should have received at least temporary vaccinations against feline distemper and rabies (if applicable in your country and if the kitten is over 12 weeks of age) and preferably protection against other major feline infections. Additionally, you should let your own vet examine your Maine Coon.

Although most owners will wish to obtain a kitten, a potential breeder or exhibitor may find that a young adult (over eight to nine months of age) is more suitable to his needs. By this age the quality of the Maine Coon is becoming more apparent. However, bear in mind that a mature Maine Coon queen will not be at her peak until she is about two years of age. A tom will be even later in reaching full maturity, and he may not peak until he is five years of age.

When selecting your Maine Coon kitten, look for one that is alert and interested in its surroundings. Owner, M. Soble and M. Thompson.

ONE OR TWO MAINE COONS?

Without any doubt, two kittens are always preferred to one. They provide constant company for each other and are a delight to watch as they play. The extra costs involved in their upkeep are unlikely to be a factor if you are able to afford a Maine Coon in the first place.

GENERAL CARE & GROOMING

In order to properly care for your Maine Coon kitten, it is advisable to purchase certain essential items before it arrives in your home. You will want at least one large litter tray. If it is too small, you will only need a bigger one later. Trays can be of the simple open style or domed to retain the odor within them. You can also purchase a litter tray curtain so that the tray is discreetly hidden yet accessible for your kitty. You will need a bag of cat litter as well.

Another essential item will be a scratching post, otherwise your cat will shred your furniture. Posts come in a range of styles—from those that are fitted to the wall to the freestanding models that can be simple or very complex climbing frames. A third essential will be a cat carrier, which can be fiberglass or of the metal cage type. Apart from being a means of transporting kitty to the vet, it also doubles as a bed and a place to confine a kitten if necessary.

You will need a soft hand brush, preferably of natural bristle not nylon, as well as one or more combs. Again, nylon is not the best choice for a comb because it generates static electricity that causes the hair to "fly." One comb should be wide-toothed, the other medium or narrow. As the kitty grows up, an extra brush of a more stiff bristle type will be required. Although it may not be needed initially, you will eventually need an elasticized cat collar and name tag.

You will also need feeding utensils: a food bowl and water bowl. There is a wide variety of them available at pet shops. Finally, your new kitten will enjoy play toys. Balls and "squeaky" mice seem to be favorites with many cats.

A scratching post is a must for every cat-owning household. It provides a cat with a rough surface on which it can hone its claws. Owner, M. Soble and M. Thompson.

SAFETY PRECAUTIONS

Before the kitten arrives in your home, check that there are no safety hazards. An open balcony is an obvious risk, as are any trailing electrical wires that are always left in their sockets. A washing machine with the door left open is a tempting place for a kitten to take a catnap. Always be careful where open doors and windows are concerned. Apart from the kitten running out if the door is an outside exit, there is the danger of doors slamming on the kitten.

that kitty will decide to climb the trailing wire and cause the iron to tumble over. All open and electrical fireplaces should, of course, be fitted with a mesh guard.

If you keep fish, be sure the tank hood is secure so that the kitten cannot knock it off and fall in the water. Indoor plants are best kept well out of kitty's reach. Apart from damaging them, some could prove poisonous if the leaves were nibbled. Any cherished ornaments should also be placed well away from a kitten.

Most cats will appreciate a nice, soft cat bed. Such accessories come in a wide variety of styles and sizes.

Be very careful when kitty is in the kitchen and you are working. They have a habit of always being under your feet as you turn round. Should you be carrying a boiling hot saucepan, this could be a real danger for you and the kitten. Likewise, never leave an iron on its board. Should you be called to the telephone, you can just bet that this will be the time

SLEEPING ARRANGEMENTS

Your kitten will be happy to sleep anywhere that is cozy, warm, and draft-free. This can be in a cat basket; its carrier, in which a soft blanket has been placed; on a chair; or best of all, on your bed. If you are the kind of person who does not look kindly on cats sleeping on your chairs or other furniture, the best advice I can give you is to forget about owning a cat!

If you wish to restrict the rooms where your cat may sleep, the simple solution is to be sure the doors are closed to those rooms. If you allow your kitten to sleep on your bed, do this only if you intend to let it do so once it is grown up; otherwise, it is unfair. Kittens really love sleeping with their owners, and they are no trouble at all—quite the opposite. They will amuse you with their antics.

toiletry needs in an already fouled litter box. Be sure fecal matter is always removed once you that see the kitten has used the litter box. Disinfect the litter box every few days so that it does not become smelly.

Litter training is accomplished simply by placing the kitten in the litter box every time it looks as though it wants to relieve itself. Such times will be whenever it wakes up, after it has eaten, and after it has been playing a while. One warning sign is the kitty

Black smoke Maine Coon about to pounce on its prey.

LITTER TRAINING

Cats are extremely clean and fastidious in all aspects of their personal habits. Kittens are easily litter box trained, providing certain fundamentals are observed. The first of these is that cats do not like to attend to their

turning in circles or searching for a corner while mewing.

Approach the kitten without alarming it and quickly transfer it to the litter box. Once this has been done on one or two occasions, the kitten will go to the litter box by itself. The main litter box is normally placed near the kitchen door. It is then a case of ensuring that it is kept clean. If the kitten roams freely indoors, you can place another litter box at a strategic point. Never admonish a kitten should it make the odd mistake, as this will prove counterproductive. Rarely will such a situation occur with a litter-trained kitten, unless the youngster is feeling ill or has loose bowels. Remember, kittens can control their bowels only for a few seconds. Total control comes, as with humans, with maturity.

Classic brown tabby Maine Coon. Owner, Judy Friedman.

GENERAL TRAINING

Cats live for the moment; they do not relate the past with the present, but draw from it via their memory to determine a course of present action. An example will illustrate this point. If you call your pet to you and then discipline it for doing something in the past, whether this was minutes before or days before, the cat will relate only to what is happening at that moment.

Any discipline imposed out of context, i.e., the time and place of the offense, will be meaningless. Any discipline must therefore occur at the moment of the misdemeanor, otherwise the two things will not be connected in the mind of your Maine Coon. If your cat is scratching the furniture, simply shout "no" if you cannot get to it and take it to the scratching post. It will associate the harsh "no" with the act of scratching the furniture, which is what you want. When you see it scratching its post, you praise it, and it will register in its mind that scratching this particular object pleases you. Training is as simple as that and only becomes difficult after a cat has been allowed to acquire bad habits.

CATS AND OTHER PETS

Kittens, in particular, will get along well with other cats and other pets if they are introduced to them at a young age. However, potential prey species are not included. Never leave a cat alone with a mouse, gerbil, hamster, small bird, baby rabbits, or guinea pigs. If it doesn't kill them, it will either maul them or frighten them. Where dogs are

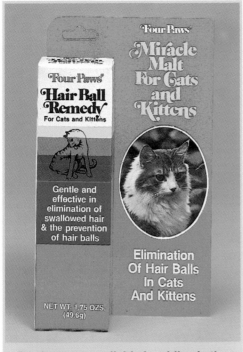

Products are available for aiding in the elimination of hairballs in cats and kittens. Photo courtesy of Four Paws.

concerned, you must watch how the dog reacts and always be present until you know they are compatible.

When kittens are introduced into a home that already has an adult cat, the cat may be curious or hostile.

However, its hostility will only take the form of spitting at the kitten or maybe cuffing it around the head with a sheathed paw. How soon it accepts the kitten can range from hours to months. Some adults will become very friendly with a kitten as it matures, others will tolerate it without ever wishing to socialize too much. Always lavish extra praise on the resident pet so that it never becomes jealous of the new interloper.

GROOMING

Daily, or at the least every other day, grooming is essential if you own a Maine Coon or any other longhaired cat. If your pet is given access to the outdoors, the coat will become tangled and matted without daily grooming. Remember, a long coat is not natural for a cat. Burrs, grasses, leaves, and any number of foreign bodies will cling to a long coat and be the source of problems. Cuts, sores, and lumps are not easily seen in a Maine Coon and can escape your attention unless you are grooming on a regular basis.

Begin as soon as you obtain your kitten. This will soon become a familiar event to the kitty. Providing you go about it in a gentle manner, it should become a pleasurable experience. Always begin by using your brush with the lie of the fur and then against it. This removes any objects in the fur and untangles the coat. Next use the wide-toothed comb. If you

Good grooming habits should start at an early age. Your pet shop can help you select the proper grooming aids for your cat. Photo courtesy of The Kong Company.

Brushing removes loose hair, stimulates the skin, and prevents the formation of mats. Owner, M. Soble and M. Thompson.

paws. In the skin, you are looking for parasites, such as fleas or lice, or for cuts and abrasions. In the paw pads, you are looking for sores or any foreign bodies that might cause an abscess. When your Maine Coon has a bath, it might be useful to have another family member help you. Be very sure that the cat has been well groomed before it is bathed; otherwise, mats will form that are better cut off. Be sure the water is only lukewarm, never hot or cold. Avoid getting shampoo in the ears or eyes. Use a shampoo formulated for cats.

Soak the hair thoroughly, then rub in the shampoo. Make sure that all the shampoo is rinsed from the coat; otherwise, it might irritate the skin when it dries. In any case, dry shampoo in the coat

feel a mat, do not pull at it but tease it apart with your fingers, then brush it, then comb again. Repeat this process until all of the hair has been groomed.

Now you can use your narrow-toothed comb to complete the grooming; do this in the same manner as with the other comb. Finish with a brisk brushing. Always take special care when combing down the legs, the tail, and the underbelly, as they are especially sensitive parts. Your pet will resent any undue pressure on them. Brush and comb the face carefully and very gently.

While grooming, take the opportunity to inspect the skin, the ears, teeth, and between the

Use guillotine-type clippers, not scissors, when clipping the claws. Be very careful not to cut into the "quick," the vein that runs through the nail.

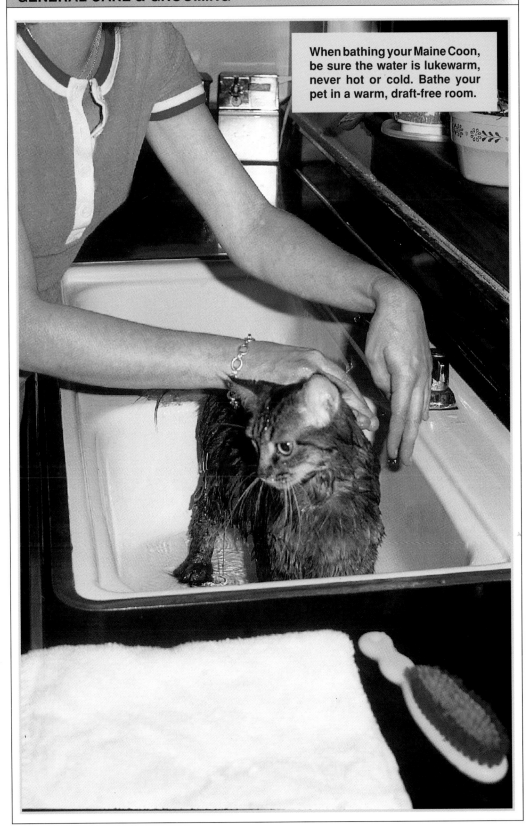

When bathing your Maine Coon, be sure the water is lukewarm, never hot or cold. Bathe your pet in a warm, draft-free room.

will make it sticky and will result in a lackluster appearance rather than a silky sheen. Finally, give the cat a brisk toweling, let it dry in a warm environment, and then groom it to remove any tangles that may have formed.

HANDLING CATS

If you have children, it is most important that they are instructed in the correct way to handle and appreciate their new pet. First of all, the kitten's privacy must be respected. Never let children wake up a sleeping kitten, because the kitty needs its sleep just as children do. Never let children play too roughly with a kitten, nor for an extended period of time. Cats like to play in short bursts. Always be sure that children never place elastic bands or string around the neck of a

kitten, and never allow children to engage in a pulling match when a kitty has hold of a piece of string. This could get caught on their fragile teeth and damage or even pull one out.

The correct way to lift a kitten is to place your hand underneath its chest. Next you can place your free hand on its neck, throat, or shoulders to secure it. It can now be lifted and firmly but gently held to your chest while the hand securing its neck will be free to stroke it. A kitten or cat must never be lifted by its front legs, nor by the loose fur on its neck. When placing a kitten back on the floor, be sure it is held securely until it is at ground level. If it feels insecure, it will try to jump. In the process it could scratch you and hurt itself if it lands awkwardly.

A Maine Coon's coat can be a perfect hiding place for fleas. Regularly check your pet for these and other parasites. Silver classic tabby with white owned by Connie Webb.

FEEDING YOUR MAINE COON

Cats and kittens are very much like people when it comes to their eating habits. Some are extremely easy to satisfy; others are much more difficult to please. Adult cats can be a worry, but at least you know they must have eaten something to have survived to maturity. Kittens, on the other hand, can prematurely turn your hair gray because you fear they may not thrive unless you can come up with some delicacy that tempts their palate!

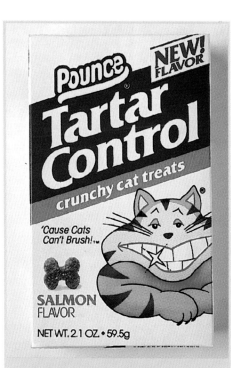

Treats can be provided on an occasional basis to help add a little variety in the diet. Some treats act as a cleansing agent to help reduce tartar on the cat's teeth. Photo courtesy of Heinz.

mammals, birds, or fish. The digestive tract of a carnivore has evolved to cope with proteins, but it has little ability to digest raw vegetable matter. This means the latter must first be boiled, so that the hard cellulose walls of such foods are softened, then broken down by the digestive juices and flora found in the alimentary tract.

In the wild, the cat would eat just about every part of its prey, leaving only the bones

Fortunately, there are so many quality brands of commercial cat foods available today that it should be possible to get even the most fastidious of kittens through its most difficult early months.

CATS ARE CARNIVORES

The cat is a prime predator in its wild habitat, and this means its basic diet must be composed of the flesh of other animals, be they

that were too large for it to digest. This diet would provide proteins and fats from the body tissues, roughage from the fur or feathers, and carbohydrates and vitamins from the partially digested vegetable matter that would be in the intestines of the prey. Combined with water, a very well-balanced diet would be provided for the cat. An equivalent of such nutrition is what you must strive to supply.

COMMERCIAL FOODS

The range of commercial cat foods encompasses canned, semi-moist, and dry diets. We have always found that our cats have never really enjoyed any of the semi-moist foods. The canned and dry foods come in an extensive range of flavors, which include meat, fish, and poultry. Of the canned foods, some have a firm consistency; others are chunks in a sauce. There are also formulated kitten foods.

Commercial foods can form the basis of your Maine Coon's diet, but you should supply a variety of them to reduce the chances that some key constituent is missing from the diet. Maine Coons will no doubt help in this matter because they seem to tire of one brand if it is fed daily. Indeed, deciding which is their chosen flavor of the week can be an interesting guessing game. They will suddenly show no interest in a product they seemed to eat with relish just a few days earlier! You will find that some cats enjoy fish flavors, others poultry and yet others, the various meats.

Dry food is enjoyed by most, though not all, Maine Coons. It provides good exercise for the teeth and jaw muscles, which canned foods do not. Their other advantage is that you can leave them out all day without their losing their appeal to your pets, or attracting flies. Water must always be available to your cats; this is even more important if the basic diet is of dried foods.

Kittens can be introduced to dry food when they reach about eight to ten weeks of age. If you have any questions about providing the proper diet, check with your vet. Owner, M. Soble and M. Thompson.

Commercial cat foods will form the basis of your Maine Coon's diet. They are available in a wide variety of flavors that are sure to please even the most finicky eater.

NON-COMMERCIAL FOODS

Your Maine Coon will enjoy many of the foods that you eat. These foods provide both variety and good exercise for the jaws. Human consumption meats can be of beef, pork, or lamb. All fish should be steamed or boiled, and it is best to stay with white fish such as cod. Tuna, sardines, and other canned fish are appreciated, but only give small quantities of them as a treat because they may prove too rich for your pet's system. Chicken is enjoyed by nearly all cats.

Cheese, egg yolk, spaghetti, and even boiled rice are all items that you can offer to your pets to see if it appeals to them. Small beef and other meat bones that still have some meat on them will be enjoyed and keep a kitten or cat amused for quite some time. Beware of bones that easily splinter, such as those of chicken or rabbit.

You can by all means see if small pieces of vegetables or fruits are accepted if mixed with the food, but generally cats will leave them. This is no problem providing that the cat is receiving commercial foods as its basic diet. Such products are all fortified with essential vitamins after the cooking process.

HOW MUCH TO FEED?

Cats prefer to eat a little but often, rather than consume one mighty meal a day. However, as carnivores, adults are well able to cope with one large meal a day. The same is not true of kittens, which should receive three or four meals per day. A kitten or a cat will normally only consume that which is needed. You can arrive at this amount by trial and error. If kitty devours its meal and is looking for more, then let it have more. You will quickly be able to judge how much each kitten needs to satisfy itself. Always remove any moist foods that are uneaten after each meal.

At 12 weeks of age the kitten should have four meals a day. One of these meals can be omitted when the kitten is 16 weeks old, but increase the quantity of the other three. You can reduce to two meals a day when the kitten is about nine months of age. From that age, it is best to continue feeding two meals—one in the morning and one in the early evening. How many times a day you feed your adult cat is unimportant. The key factor is that it receives as much as it needs over the day, and that the diet is balanced to provide the essential ingredients discussed earlier. It is also better that meals are given regularly. Cats, like humans, are creatures of habit.

WATER

If a cat's diet is essentially of moist foods, it will drink far less than if the diet is basically of dry foods. Many cats do not like faucet (tap) water because they are able to smell and taste the many additives included by your local water board. Chlorine is high on this list. Although it dissipates into the air quite readily, chloromides do not, which is why the cat may ignore the water. During the filtering process at the water station, chemicals are both taken out and added. The resulting mineral balance and taste are often not to a cat's liking. This is why you will see cats drinking from puddles, a flower vase, or even your toilet, because the taste is better for them. If your water is refused, then you can see if your cat prefers mineralized bottled water—not distilled because the latter has no mineral content to it.

THE NEW ARRIVAL

It is a very traumatic time for a kitten when it leaves its mother and siblings. It will often eat well the first day; however, as it starts to miss its family, it will fret. You can reduce its stress by providing the diet it was receiving from the seller. You can change the diet slowly, if necessary, as it settles down. Of course, many kittens have no problems, but if yours does, this feeding advice should help its period of adjustment.

What is essential is that the kitten takes in sufficient liquids so that it does not start to dehydrate. This, more than anything else, will adversely affect its health very rapidly. If you are at all concerned, do consult your vet. The kitten may have picked up a virus, but if it is treated

promptly, this should not be a problem. Your vet might supply you with a dietary supplement, which we have found excellent for kittens experiencing "new home syndrome."

Clean fresh water should be available at all times.

KEEPING YOUR MAINE COON HEALTHY

Like any other animal, your Maine Coon can fall victim to hundreds of diseases and conditions. Most can be prevented by sound husbandry. The majority, should they be recognized in their early stages, can be treated with modern drugs or by surgery. Clearly, preventive techniques are better and less costly than treatments, yet in many instances a cat will become ill because the owner has neglected some basic aspect of general management. In this chapter, we are not so much concerned with cataloging all the diseases your cat could contract, because these are legion, but more concerned with reviewing sound management methods.

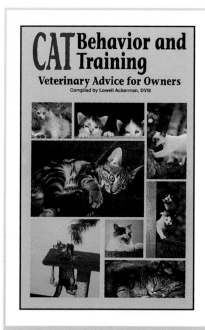

T.F.H. Publications, the world's largest publisher of pet animal books, offers a large selection of books about cats and their care.

HYGIENE

Always apply routine hygiene to all aspects of your pet's management. This alone dramatically reduces the chances of your pet becoming ill because it restricts pathogens (disease- causing organisms) from building up colonies that are able to overcome the natural defense mechanisms of your Maine Coon.

1. After your cat has eaten its fill of any moist foods, either discard the food or keep it for later by placing it in your refrigerator. Anything left uneaten at the end of the day can be trashed. Always wash the bowl after each meal. Do not feed your pet from any dishes that are chipped, cracked, or, in the case of plastic, those that are badly scratched.

2. Always store food in a dry, cool cupboard or in the refrigerator in the case of fresh foods.

3. For whatever reason, if you have been handling someone else's cats, always wash your hands before handling your own cats.

4. Be rigorous in cleaning your cat's litter box as soon as you see that it has been fouled.

5. Pay particular attention to the grooming of a Maine Coon cat because so many problems can begin with a seemingly innocuous event. For example, in itself, a minor cut may not be a major problem as long as it is treated with an antiseptic. But if it is left as an open untreated wound, it is an obvious site for bacterial colonization. The bacteria then gain access to the bloodstream, and a major problem ensues that might not even be associated with the initial wound. The same applies to flea or lice bites. Inspect the skin carefully for signs of flea droppings when you groom a Maine Coon. These appear like minute specks of black dust.

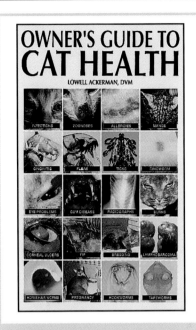

OWNER'S GUIDE TO CAT HEALTH

LOWELL ACKERMAN, DVM

T.F.H. cat health books are written by veterinarians who are specialists in their fields.

muscle by jumping and landing awkwardly. This would normally correct itself over a 36-48 hour period. Your pet may contract a slight chill, or its feces might become loose. Both conditions will normally correct themselves over a day or so. On the other hand, if a condition persists for more than two days, it would be advisable to telephone your vet for advice.

In general, any appearance or behavior that is not normal for your cat would suggest something is responsible for the abnormality. This is your first indication that something may be amiss. The following are a number of signs that indicate a problem:

1. Diarrhea, especially if it is very liquid, foul-smelling or blood-streaked. If blood is seen in the urine, this is also an indication of a problem, as is excessive straining or cries of pain when the cat tries to relieve itself.

RECOGNIZING AN ILL CAT

You must be able to recognize when your cat is ill in order to seek a solution to the problem. You must learn to distinguish between a purely temporary condition and that which will need some form of veterinary advice and/or treatment. For example, a cat can sprain a

2. Discharge from the nose or eyes. Some breeds of cat may experience this condition more than others.

Excessive discharge requires veterinary attention.

3. Repeated vomiting. All cats are sick occasionally with indigestion. They will also vomit after eating grass, but repeated vomiting is not normal.

4. Wheezing sounds when breathing, or any other suggestion of breathing difficulties.

5. Excessive scratching. All cats will have a good scratch on a quite regular basis, but excessive scratching indicates a skin problem, especially if it has created sores or lesions.

6. Constant rubbing of the rear end along the ground.

7. Bald patches, lesions, cuts, and swellings on the body, legs, tail, or face.

8. The coat seems to lack bounce or life, and is dull.

9. The cat is listless and lethargic, showing little interest in what is going on around it.

10. The eyes have a glazed look to them, or the haw (nictitating membrane, or third eyelid) is clearly visible.

11. The cat is displaying an unusual lack of interest in its favorite food items.

12. The gums of the teeth seem very red or swollen.

13. Fits or other abnormal signs of behavior.

14. Any obvious pain or distress.

Very often two or more clinical signs will be apparent when a condition is developing. The number of signs increases as the disease or ailment advances to a more sinister stage.

Like all other cats, Maine Coons can be subject to ear mites. If the ears are foul smelling or if you notice a dark, waxy substance, consult your vet. Such conditions are not uncommon and are easily treatable.

DIAGNOSIS

Correct diagnosis is of the utmost importance before any form of treatment can be administered. Often it will require blood and/or fecal microscopy in order to establish the exact cause of a condition. Many of the signs listed above are common to most diseases, so never attempt home diagnosis and treatment: if you are wrong, your cherished Maine Coon may pay for your error with its life. Once ill health is suspected, any lost time favors the pathogens and makes treatment both more difficult and more costly.

In making your original decision to purchase a Maine Coon, or any other cat, you should always have allowed for the cost of veterinary treatment. If this is likely to be a burden that you cannot afford, then do not purchase a cat. The first few months, and especially the first weeks, is the time when most cats will become ill. If they survive this period, the chances are that future visits to the vet will be rare, other than for booster vaccinations.

Kittens do not have the immunity to pathogens that the adult cat does, nor do they have the muscle reserves of the adult. If they are ill, they need veterinary help very quickly if they are to have a good chance of overcoming a disease or major problem.

Having decided that your cat is not well, you should make notes on paper of the signs of the problem, when you first noticed them, and how quickly things have deteriorated. If possible, obtain a fecal and urine sample, then telephone your vet and make an appointment. Ask other cat owners in your area who their vet

T.F.H. cat health and cat care books are available at pet shops everywhere.

is. Some vets display a greater liking for cats, or dogs, or horses than do others. This is just human nature, but obviously you want to go to one that has a special affection for felines.

TREATMENT

Once your vet has prescribed a course of treatment, it is important that you follow it exactly as instructed. Do not discontinue the medicine because the cat shows a big improvement. Such an action could prove counterproductive, and the pathogens that had not been killed might develop an immunity to the treatment. A relapse could occur, and this might be more difficult to deal with.

VACCINATIONS

There are a few extremely dangerous diseases that afflict cats, but fortunately there are vaccines that can dramatically reduce the risk of them infecting your Maine Coon. The bacteria and viruses that cause such diseases are often found in the air wherever there are cats. Discuss a program of immunization with your vet.

When a kitten is born, it inherits protection from disease via the colostrum of its mother's milk. Such protection may last for up to 16 weeks—but it varies from kitten to kitten and may last only six weeks. It is therefore recommended that your kitten be vaccinated against diseases at six to eight weeks of age just to be on the safe side. Boosters are required some weeks later and thereafter each year. Potential breeding females should be given boosters about three to four weeks prior to the due date. This will ensure that a high level of antibodies is passed to the kittens.

An important consideration with regard to the major killer diseases in cats is the treatment of infection. If a cat survives an infection, it will probably be a carrier of the disease and shed the pathogens continually throughout its life. The only safe course is therefore to ensure that your kittens are protected. The main diseases for which there are vaccinations are as follows:

Rabies: This is a disease of the neurological system. It is non-existent in Great Britain, Ireland, Australia, New Zealand, Hawaii, certain oceanic islands, Holland, Sweden, and Norway. In these countries, extremely rigid quarantine laws are applied to ensure it stays that way. You cannot have your cat vaccinated against rabies if you live in one of these countries, unless you are about to emigrate with your cat. In all other countries, rabies vaccinations are either compulsory or strongly advised. They are given when the kitten is three or more months of age.

Feline panleukopenia: Also known as feline infectious enteritis, and feline distemper. This is a highly contagious viral disease. Vaccinations are given when the kitten is about eight weeks old, and a booster is given four weeks later. In high-risk areas, a third injection may be advised four weeks after the second one.

Feline respiratory disease complex: Often referred to as cat flu but this is incorrect. Although a number of diseases are within this group, two of them are especially dangerous. They are feline viral rhinotracheitis (FVR) and feline calicivirus (FCV). The vaccination for the prevention of these diseases is combined and given when the kitten is six or more weeks of age; a booster follows three to four weeks later.

Feline leukemia virus complex (FeLV): This disease was first recognized in 1964, and a vaccine became available in the US in about 1985. Like "cat flu," the name is misleading, because it is far more complex than a blood cancer, which is what its name implies. Essentially, it destroys the cat's immune system, so the cat may contract any of the major diseases.

The disease is easily spread via the saliva of a cat as it licks other cats. It is also spread prenatally from an infected queen to her offspring via the blood, or when washing her kittens. This is why it is important to test all breeding cats for FeLV. Vaccination is worthwhile only on a kitten or cat that has tested negative. If a cat tests positive for the disease, it has a 70 percent chance of survival, though it will be a carrier in many instances.

Feline infectious peritonitis (FIP): This disease has various effects on the body's metabolism. There are no satisfactory tests for it, but intranasal liquid vaccinations via a dropper greatly reduce the potential for it to develop in the tissues of the nose.

PARASITES

Parasites are organisms that live on or in a host. They feed from it without providing any benefit in return. External parasites include fleas, lice, ticks, flies, and any other creature that bites the skin of the cat. Internal parasites include all pathogens, but the term is more commonly applied to worms in their various forms.

External parasites and their eggs can be seen with the naked eye. All can be eradicated with treatment from your vet. However, initial treatment will need to be

Cats that are allowed outdoors are particularly susceptible to parasitic infestation by fleas, lice, and ticks.

followed by further treatments because most compounds are ineffective on the eggs. The repeat treatments kill the larvae as they hatch. It is also important that all bedding be treated or destroyed because this is often where parasites prefer to live when not on the host.

All cats are host to a range of worm species. If worms multiply in the cat, they adversely affect its health. They will cause loss of appetite, wasting, and a steady deterioration in health. At a high level of infestation, they may be seen in the fecal matter, but normally it will require fecal microscopy by your vet. This will establish the species and the relative density of the eggs, thus the level of infestation.

Treatment is normally via tablets, but liquids are also available. Because worms are so common, the best husbandry technique is to routinely treat breeding cats for worms prior to their being bred, then for the queen and her kittens to be treated periodically. Discuss a testing and treatment program with your vet.

NEUTERING AND SPAYING

Desexing your cat is normally done when a female is about four months of age and somewhat later with a male. The operation is quite simple with a male but more complicated with a female. It is still a routine procedure. It is possible to delay estrus in a breeding queen, but the risk of negative side effects makes this a dubious course to take. Discuss it with your vet. A cat of any age can be neutered (male) or spayed (female); but if they are adults, they take some months (especially males) before they lose their old habits.

Maine Coon queen and her eight-week-old kittens. Owner, M. Soble and M. Thompson.

FIRST AID

Although you might think that such inquisitive creatures as cats would be prone to many physical injuries, this is not actually the case. They usually extricate themselves from dangerous situations because of their very fast reflexes. However, injuries do happen, and the most common is caused by the cat darting across a road and being hit by a vehicle. About 40 percent of cats die annually due to traffic accidents. The next level of injury will be caused by cats getting bitten or scratched when fighting among themselves, or being bitten by an insect, or by a sharp object getting lodged in their fur or feet.

If your cat is hit by a vehicle, the first thing to do is to try and place it on a board of some sort and remove it to a safe place. Do not lift its head because this might result in it swallowing blood into the lungs. Try to keep it calm by talking soothingly to it.

If the cat is still mobile, but has clearly been badly hurt, you must try and restrict its movements by wrapping it in a blanket or towel. If it is bleeding badly, try to contain the flow by wrapping a bandage around the body or leg to reduce the blood loss. With a minor cut, you should trim the hair away from the wound, bathe it, then apply an antiseptic or stem the flow with a styptic pencil or other coagulant.

If you suspect that your cat has been bitten by an insect and the result is a swelling, the poison is already in the skin so external ointments will have virtually no effect. The same is true of an abscess caused by fighting. The only answer is to let your vet use surgery to lance and treat the wound.

If you are determined to give your Maine Coon the opportunity to be outdoors, a secure outdoor enclosure is your safest option. Owner, Frederick O. Duane.

Fortunately, cats rarely swallow poison because they are such careful eaters. In all instances, immediately contact your vet and advise him of the kind of poison the cat has consumed.

If your cat should ever be badly frightened, for example, by a dog chasing and maybe biting it, the effect of this may not be apparent immediately. It may go into shock some time later. Keep the cat indoors so that you can see how it reacts. Should it go into shock and collapse, place a blanket around it and take it to the vet. If this is not possible, place it in a darkened room and cover it with a blanket so it does not lose too much body heat. Comfort it until you can make contact with the vet.

EXHIBITING MAINE COONS

From the first time cats were seriously exhibited in London in 1871, the cat show has been the very heart of the fancy. It is the place where breeders can have the merits of their stock assessed in a competitive framework, where all cat lovers can meet and discuss ideas, trends and needs, and where new products for cats can be promoted. It is the only event in which you have the opportunity of seeing just about every color and pattern variety that exists in the Maine Coon breed.

Even if you have no plans to become a breeder or exhibitor, you should visit at least one or two cat shows to see what a quality Maine Coon looks like.

TYPES OF SHOW

Shows range from the small informal affairs that attract a largely local entry to the major all-breed championships and specialty exhibitions that can be spread over two or more days (but only one in Britain). A specialty is a show restricted either by breed or by hair length (short or long). In the US, it is quite common for two or more shows to run concurrently at the same site.

SHOW CLASSES

The number of classes staged at a given show will obviously reflect its size, but the classes fall into various major divisions. These are championships for whole cats, premierships for altered cats, open classes for both of the previous cats, kittens, and household pets. In all but the pet class, there are separate classes for males and females. There are then classes for all of the color and pattern varieties. At a small show, the color/patterns may be grouped into fewer classes than at a major show.

All classes are judged against the standard for the breed, other than pet classes, in which the exhibits are judged on the basis of condition and general appeal, or uniqueness of pattern. An unregistered Maine Coon can be entered into a pet class, and it will be judged on the same basis as would a mixed breed. A kitten in the US is a cat of four months of age but under eight months on the day of a show. In Britain a kitten is a cat of three or more months and under nine months on the show day.

AWARDS AND PRIZES

The major awards in cats are those of Champion and Grand Champion, Premier and Grand Premier. In Britain, a cat must win three challenge certificates under different judges to become a champion, while in the US it must win six winner's ribbons. In both instances, these awards are won via the open class. Once a cat is a champion, it then competes in the champions' class and becomes a grand based on points earned in defeating other champions. The prizes can range from certificates, ribbons and cups to trophies and cash.

Wins in kitten classes do not count toward champion status. Champion status in one association does not carry over to another, in which a cat would have to win its title again based on the rules of that association. The rules of competition are complex, and any would-be exhibitor should obtain a copy of them from their particular registry.

Many Maine Coon fanciers find exhibiting to be the most exciting aspect of the hobby.

The general format of cat shows, while differing somewhat from one country to another, is much the same in broad terms. A Maine Coon will enter its color or pattern class. If it wins, it will progress to compete against other group winners in its breed, and ultimately compete for best of breed. If classes have been scheduled for all of the recognized colors and patterns in all of the recognized breeds, then a Best in Show will be the ultimate award. This is the dream of every cat exhibitor.

JUDGING

As stated earlier, cats are judged against their written standard rather than against each other. A winning cat is one that records the highest total of points, or, put another way, the least number of demerit marks. In the US cats are taken to the judge's table for assessment, but in Britain the judge moves around the pens with a trolley. In the US, judging is done in front of the public, but in the UK judging is normally done before the public is allowed into the hall. The exhibit owners are requested to leave the hall during judging.

CAT PENS

When you arrive at the cat show, a pen will be allocated to your cat. This is an all-wire cage. In Britain, the rules governing what can be placed into the cage are very rigid. This is because there can be no means of identifying the owner of the cat when the judge arrives at that pen. Thus, the blanket, the litter box and the water vessel must all be white. In the US the pens are highly decorated with silks, gorgeous cushions, and so on because the cat is taken to another pen for judging.

THE EXHIBITION MAINE COON

Obviously, a Maine Coon show cat must be a very sound example of its breed. Its coat must be in truly beautiful condition because the level of competition is extremely high at the major

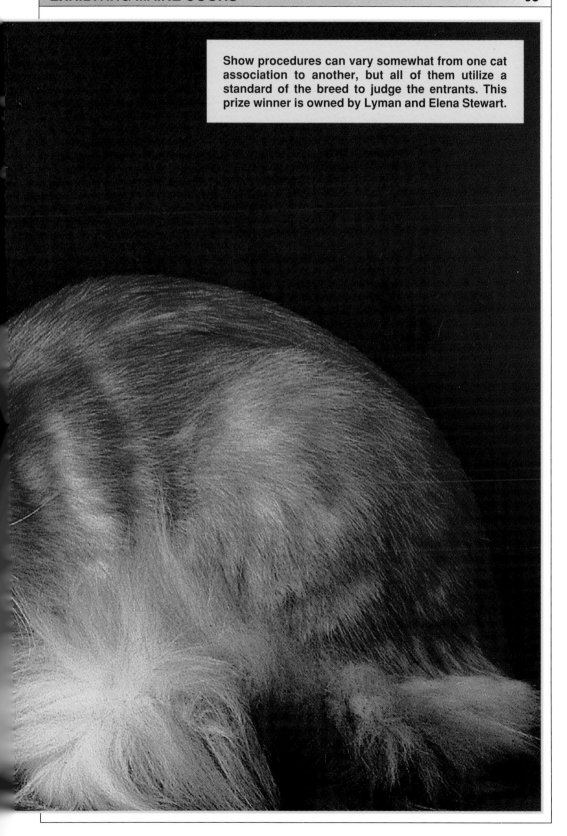

Show procedures can vary somewhat from one cat association to another, but all of them utilize a standard of the breed to judge the entrants. This prize winner is owned by Lyman and Elena Stewart.

events. At more local affairs, the quality will not be as high, which gives more exhibitors a chance to pick up victories in the absence of the top cats of the country. The male cat must have two descended testicles and have a valid vaccination certificate against feline enteritis that was issued at least seven days before the show. It should have tested negative for feline leukemia (and/or any other diseases as required by your registry).

Tabby Maine Coon kitten. A cat carrier such as the one shown here enables you to transport your pet safely and comfortably. Owner, Susan E. Shaw.

A show cat must be well-mannered because if it should bite or claw the judge, it is hardly likely to win favor. It could even be disqualified, depending on the regulations of your registry. In any case, such a cat could not be examined properly by the judge, so this alone would preclude it from any hope of winning. It must therefore become accustomed to such treatment by being handled very often as a kitten.

ENTERING A SHOW

You must apply to the show secretary for an entry blank and a schedule. The secretary will list the classes and state the rules of that association. The entry form must be completed and returned, with fees due, by the last date of entry as stipulated for that show. It is very important that you enter the correct classes; otherwise, your cat will be eliminated and your fee forfeited. If you are unsure about this aspect, you can seek the advice of an exhibitor of your acquaintance, or simply call the show secretary.

SHOW ITEMS

When attending a show you will need a variety of items. They include a cat carrier, litter box, blankets, food and water vessels, food, your cat's own supply of your local water if necessary, disinfectant, first aid kit, grooming tools, paper towels, entry pass, vaccination certificates, show catalog to check the entry for your cat and when it is likely to be judged, a small stool, and decorations for the pen. You may also wish to take your own food. Indeed, it would be wise to invest in a collapsible cart to transport all of the above!

The best advice is that you should visit shows and talk with exhibitors so that you can get the feel of things before you make the plunge yourself. Showing is a fascinating and thoroughly addictive pastime, but it is also time-consuming, can be costly, and entails a great deal of dedication. Fortunately, you can participate to whatever level you wish. You are also assured of making many new friends.

INDEX